PUBLIC DREAM

Frances Leviston was born in Edinburgh in 1982 and later moved to Sheffield. She read English at St Hilda's College, Oxford, and has an MA in Writing from Sheffield Hallam University. A pamphlet of her work, *Lighter*, was published in 2004 by Mews Press, and became the PBS Bulletin's Pamphlet Choice for Spring 2005. Her poems have appeared in various magazines and anthologies including *New Writing 14*, *Poetry Review*, *Poetry London*, *Ten Hallam Poets* and the *TLS*. She received an Eric Gregory Award in 2006.

T0371011

PUBLIC DREAM

Frances Leviston

PICADOR

First published 2007 by Picador
an imprint of Pan Macmillan
20 New Wharf Road, London N1 9RR
Associated companies throughout the world
www.panmacmillan.com

ISBN 978-0-330-44054-7

A CIP catalogue record for this book is available from
the British Library.

Designed by Macmillan Design Department

Visit **www.picador.com** to read more about all our books
and to buy them. You will also find features, author interviews and
news of any author events, and you can sign up for e-newsletters
so that you're always first to hear about our new releases.

for my parents

Acknowledgements are due to the editors of the following publications, in which some of these poems first appeared: the *Frogmore Papers*, *New Writing 14*, *Pennine Platform*, *Poetry London*, *Poetry Review*, *The Red Wheelbarrow*, the *Times Literary Supplement*, *Tower Poets*, and *The Weevil*. A number of these poems were also published in *Lighter* (Mews Press, 2004) and *Ten Hallam Poets* (Mews Press, 2005).

Thanks to Sean O'Brien, Don Paterson, Simon Pomery, Russ Willey, JFNG, and all the other friends and family who have given their advice and encouragement. Thanks, also, to the Society of Authors for their support.

CONTENTS

PUBLIC DREAM

HUMBLES

If you have hit a deer on the road at dusk;
climbed, shivering, out of your car
with curses to investigate the damage
done, and found it split apart and steaming
far-flung in the nettle bed, utterly beyond repair,
then you have seen what is not meant to be seen,
is packed in cannily, coiled, like parachute silks,
but unputbackable, out for the world to witness:
the looping, slicked-up clockspring
flesh's pink, mauve, arterial red,
and there a still-pulsing web of royal veins
bearing the bad news back to the heart;
something broken, something hard, black,
the burst bowel fouling the meat
exposed for what it is, found out – as Judas,
ripped from groin to gizzard, was found
at dawn, on the elder tree, still tethered to earth
by all the ropes and anchors of his life.

I RESOLVE TO LIVE CHASTELY

and hurry home, carrying my shoes through empty
precincts as the morning darkens. I thought I'd make it
before the wheel of cloud came round
but I'm only on the corner when the heavens begin
to spit like a pack of disapproving old women,

so here I am sheltering under the lintel of St Mary's
church, I'll thank you not to laugh, waiting
for the shower to pass me over, with blistered bare feet,
what you get for wearing inhumanly pointed
heels that tie with black ribbon round the ankle

and dancing all night in the name of nothing
noble – not the *corps de ballet* bleeding splendour
as they assume the positions of true love
for a paying audience, though I did ask
his name, but I've lost it again. The weather vane

pirouettes. I'm thinking of the girl with no breasts
who ate sweet pepper first, so she could tell
when to stop throwing up. I want to know who
she imagined was counting, for whom the red stain
was atonement, for what. I want to know

what keeps me here, back to the grille, searching
for a dry foot of ground, in sight of all those beads
of water sliding down a stem of grass. What else is it
for, my skin, if not this pelting, streaming world?

FEAR

The crackle that pulled
the darkness tight

was the sound of the rose
on my bureau, unfolding.

VIEW OF A TREE

Watching a tree as it blows with the wind
for long enough, the air in the mind

grows stiller, still, and the wind's a shudder
rising where the tap-root draws the water

in blindness, on the other side of bark,
to sound the greenest ring of the heart

as breath produces notes along a pipe,
through every branch, to every sharp leaf-tip,

till the whole lot bows, and dances, and nods.
Of course it wasn't the will of the gods

that Orpheus should play – he played to please –
or that each maenad watching from the trees

should stone him, and then, when the stones flew wide,
with her own red hands rip free his head:

something sings in the river's blackness
that isn't a tide. We make our chances

far from the mercy of weather, or man.
I hold this view for as long as I can.

FIREWALKER

If you ask me to choose – and God knows choice
should not show its tricksy face here, today,
in the hot church of conviction – I'll tell you

Joan of Arc, who I sometimes see
heading the school bus stampede at three thirty,
her little knot of loyals behind her

desperate to find such confidence
(let's not forget, Joan was barely twelve when it started),
I'll tell you: she was blessed. And that means

more than you or I can hope for,
muddling through the alleys to work, blanking beggars
or begging ourselves; blessed with visions,

which are light, slanting through a small, high window
into a room that has no door,
where time and colour mean little or nothing

and one sees only shape, as when a girl on a pyre
burns clear of particulars, the skin's crack, the spit
and slob of fat along the thigh,

to darken as a girl again, fixed like that
on her stage of fire. But say the room has no window.
Say you have to live

by whatever flicker you coax yourself
from splinters and scraps, and books, if needs must
(*the barbarity!* they cry, as if a stripped spine is worse) –

what then? When they are burning
Joan again, until there is nothing but a twist of French bone
and the scent of her frightful hair, I remember,

because there is nowhere else to go,
that tonight, in Jakarta, a man emerges whole
from the shimmering trench of coals,

his dhoti a cloud, his body raining
the gentle, unromantic rain that martyrs reject
for their desert of truth – he is emerging,

his blood hanging on to the heat like a brand
and the crowd's drum pounding in favour of life,
and survival, and life, and life.

ATHEIST LIGHTING A CANDLE IN ALBI CATHEDRAL

i.m. Tyler Kelley

It seems to matter
I use a Zippo,
not the taper's monkish flame.

It seems to matter I choose the white
over red before asking the difference,

that I love the fresco's talented horse
though couldn't name his rider –

but what's not authentic at the Virgin's feet?
She knows I am not a bad person, just troubled.
She knows the wick is burning.

FOLEGANDROS

The wind is lonely.
It cannot be real
at sea, it cannot confirm itself
but rushes about
until it encounters witnesses.
The island's tiers,
a fence post to rub against,
olive trees, billy goats,
and human inhabitants
break it. Now
it is always arriving.
Tired at times
it falls to a murmur,
moving the dust from leaf to leaf,
then rises at night,
afraid it cannot see itself
or anything else, afraid
the world has vanished forever.
There is a childish
feel to its always being there,
how it follows and whines,
how it interrupts
your private moments
taken on the beach at dusk.
You wish for a god
you could ask to appease it,
some rite,
some ritual sacrifice

to quiet its roaring and lull
it to sleep,
but there is nothing
left you believe in –
only the wind
filling the domes of summit churches
and donkeys' ears,
dying at last
in the maze of your lungs.

DRAGONFLIES

Watching these dragonflies
couple in air, or watching them try,
the slender red wands
of their bodies tapped
end to end, then faltering wide
on the currents of what feels to me
a fairly calm day,

I think of delicate clumsinesses
lovers who have not yet mentioned
love aloud enact,
the shy hands they extend
then retract, the luscious fumbled chase
among small matters seeming massive
as rushes are to dragonflies,

and in the accidental
buzz of a dragonfly against bare skin,
how one touch fires
one off again on furious wings
driven towards love and love, in its lightness,
driven the opposite way,

so in fact they hardly meet
but hang in the hum of their own desires.
Still, who would ask
these dragonflies to land on a stone
and like two stones to consummate?
How can I demand love stop, and speak?

EGGS AND CASTLES

When you held that half a hatched white shell
you found inside the blackening spiral
of the castle's fallen keep to my ear
and crackled the broken bits that still clung
fluttering on the membrane together
I heard how the bird heard, for the first time

wind rustling the moat full of thistles
moonlight cows in the pasture tearing grass
from the high ridge road a distant motor
reverberating off the ruined walls
and the vain cry of the manor's peacock
piercing lake and dark like a polished claw

that wakes the now-dream into another
each more fresh and closer than the last
Trembling in that empty cup of air
I could have believed consciousness began
in your hands, that from your hands issued forth
all thistles, all castles, all horizons

INDUSTRIAL

From a bridge, the inverted *vanitas*
Of a swan drifting down a black canal
Between two corrugated warehouses.

UNTHINKABLE

I dreamed I was afraid to walk between the tower blocks
that stand on the hill to the west of this city, I was afraid
of the pissed-in stairwells, each a hollow of fallen leaves
and the hanging wires and the ceiling tiles' asbestos
and the clatter and squeak of pushchairs down the walkway

I was afraid of the people inside, trapped like spiders in a sink
neither rescued nor put out of what I imagined to be
their misery, the mean-lipped girls shaking gold charms
and blitz-blonde hair, the men with twisted caps and
    teeth and business
to attend to *don't you speak like that to me you slag I'll break
    your fucking jaw*

I was afraid of silence, of shrieks banging against each other
no halfway house between the two, of the organs and
    the skin, starved
thighs like whippets', all bone and shank, I was afraid of
    splinters, of everything
broken but gripping strong as a dead dog's bite, and of there
being no doctors here

but when I woke in the master bedroom I could still hear
the cry from the sixth-floor harpy at dusk, which is the
    same long cry
that sails from the pigeon coops across the valley
where tenderness is not unthinkable, and I understood the
    terrible coughing
in the shut room was laughter, and that love – love! –
    answered, came

in from the cold each night, hands shoved in pockets,
unspeakable, so much the fiercer for that

LAMPADROME

Lampadedromy n. (Gr. Antiq.)
A torch-race . . . 1848 Craig has the
incorrect form Lampadrome . . .
– OED

It's late, but here's the linkboy's light for hire.
He lifts it, dripping, high above his head,
and waits his corner, watching textures fade,
night flood the streets from its reservoir

submerging Corinth, and the men who pass
for a trading empire's living idols
in fur-lined cloaks and new leather sandals
grow nervous enough to approach him first.

There is a tremor inside their demands
for guidance – they know their silver palms
are dull as an abandoned temple's alms
without the benefaction of his brand,

which, with careless alchemy, transmutes
their muted coins and greying hair to gold.
Despite his advantage, he's still compelled
to mark the sought address and pick their route,

squeezing with awful calm through a dark door
his torch reveals to be the road, unpaved,
between the walls of housing so deprived
his passengers, for all they can be sure,

have shifted planes. They cling to the light,
not so much afraid of what they witness
as what their sudden consciences can guess –
the thieves and whores, the madman's single note –

must somewhere now be living, since they don't
appear to breathe the rest of Corinth's air.
Beyond the open doorway of a bar
full cups lie smashed, and women creak with want,

and some rough answer's blowing down the street.
The boy's a marvel! Completely unafraid,
and honest, too: his fee already paid,
he could – no loss – have left them there for meat,

but now they spill like syrup from a tap
and find they're on a thoroughfare they know,
carrying them round the lampadrome
past fans who press and crane at every gap.

Our boy is one. The merchants never guess
that every fare he's taken passed this way,
no matter what the risk, what loop awry
to skirt the roaring, monolithic mass

and through those columns' black interstices
to glimpse a distant nimbus – five, or six,
now clumped, now stringing out and out, like tricks
on the eyes – distending in a breeze

and lapping glory: fickle, minor gods
disguised at play, and each one's brazier hitched
to an athlete lit and lofted from the pitch
of obscurity – like Aaron's rod,

its roadside yellow flowers blazing high
to lead the funeral march through any map.
Applause unfolds inside, that sticky trap.
He'd like to run the race before he dies

or die right now, his unsung torch nipped out
and silver gone to get some bastard pissed.
What difference is there – linkboy, lampadist?
The one who burns within, the one without.

GROTTOES

Though we came for the cave-painted
mammoth, the auroch, the ochre-haloed
hand above a pony's rump,

and the contour made to stand as a muzzle,
proof that man has always looked for
one thing prisoned in the sap of another,

though we came with our cameras hunting for it,
a cave-pearl accruing in a rusty basin,
a child's footprint remembered by mud,

bones tumbled in a bear-scratch
as if he might at any moment
shamble back in,

what we brought to the surface was the farthest cave
where the roped path circles back on itself,
the lights finish, and a swag of roots

drop fine and gold from the roof
to the floor: the future, lonely
as a girl in a tower, letting down her hair.

IN THE DAGUERREOTYPES

Like a disowned daughter you
escaped the ancestor's weight,
physiognomy, costuming,

but here they suddenly
are: galleried, frowning into suffrage,
bottle curls dropping.
Someone is typing documents
with awful gusto, concentrating

towards a tomorrow
under bronze firmaments,
marriage: men, wives, lacework,
dolls. Is a sled standing
still, tarmacadam under snow-drift,

now you cannot unacquaint
the faces tarnished
with fantasy? Not by whatever
began. By what continued.

TWO SILENCES

1

Soft, feathered stirrings in the dovecote;
a quirk of napes, a distinction of quills,
in the slats of light the clapboard walls –
no matter how well-made, how dove-tailed –
admit, their suggestion of prison bars;
airs warmed and displaced as water
poured off the bath to discover a form:
a number given, their quickness covered,
their whiteness understood despite the dark.

2

The kids are doing sponsored silences.
In the prim mouths, the ascetic looks,
there is some reproach. Or is it in me,
when one by one they forget themselves
and return to the natural condition
of noise, that I wish they had listened
more to the world, and questioned less; I wish
for myself an excuse to be silent,
or if I speak, to speak from some duress?

TO ALL INTENTS AND PURPOSES

I have struggled all my life to never
write about the pepper mill

its corset shape
of common wood
and secret machinery goings-on
of grinding, grinding kernels down to drift
like ash from a chimney

but now I am lamed in the kitchen
now winter slants a window frosted shut
because it knows I am alone
I find it's not a paperweight, not even a Christmas rose
in my right hand, but the pepper mill
lifting to my nose like a snuff-box

There is not a breath that doesn't burn
with the invisible

One spring my father's father sank a pipe
and gassed the warren
His men with shotguns stood by
every freshly blasted burrow-mouth, taking turns
to roll a smoke
until the sun had set
                        So many houses
built on ground like this – the offices and factories
and mills where lines of women work a loom
to thread the rotten cloth, rags
across their mouths that let them breathe

and I had not seen until now, I had forgotten
how clear the grain is running through the brown wood
how shy the hourglass shape
and the stamp you are never supposed to read
on the base of the pestle, spinning in the dark drum
Cole & Mason, England –
                              here is my mother
buying her goods from *respectable companies*
blowing the dust from a tinned Yule pudding
then putting it back on the shelf

I am holding the mill too tightly, I know
if the man comes now he will think I am one of those
women whose fingers need prising off things
the milkman, the postman
the window-cleaner wanting notes
might find me here
still barefoot in my dressing gown
and breathing down a hot black hum

how the raw side of a coffin smells
how the scorch of a gun would taste
at the rim of the mouth, would burn
on the back of the tongue

THE REPRIEVE

They said we should be glad to be spared
given what we'd crawled from under, given the heaps,
the sodden piles we'd hidden under, what we'd stood up in
hours later, bone-cold and wet to the skin.

We passed a stubble field where a boy lay sleeping
somewhere near home. He'd left a few stalks of wheat
    still standing
when the blade and the handle parted ways. We watched
    them shiver,
newly exposed to the northerly wind, and the birds gather,
no gunshot or handclap to shoo them away.

FRANCO'S GARDEN

It was no secret,
but we are nevertheless surprised
to enter this garden
behind the rows of rusted cannons, parapets
that keep their warmth
until they are sure of morning again.
Hedges and vines,
the bright, soft tissues of climbing roses,
reach towards the sun.
Branches cross and uncross.
A half-wild cat
is clawing the bark off an almond tree.
We will never get to the bottom of this.
The roots of the plants and the prison's foundations
are tangled under the earth.

EVERY ANIMAL HAS A NOISE EXCEPT US

August
and the lambs
have been taken from the mothers.
All day they cast their human cries
across the field-fence, into the pond of a farmer's ear
and down through mud to the never-forgotten
need to tell of what was lost –
the gut-fished, unrefusable tongue,
the sunken tongue,
the loss.

OILSEED RAPE

Americans call it *canola* oil, the upshot of this
almost incredibly yellow horizon

charging the clouds, like a buttercup
held close to the chin

tells if you like butter or not. And then it's gone
along with most of the profitable land

when the flyover's fled, and what remains
is the blot of a stared-at sun on the eye,

those thousands and thousands of blonde girls
bowing their heads.

INCUBUS

I've heard of it happening to other women
And other women say they've heard it happens
But thought it could not happen to them,
Or that, if it did, they would fight for justice
Whatever it took, and I've heard of it taking
Several years to come to nothing,
Several years along with the rest.
Since it happened to me, I've heard me saying
I'd heard this sort of thing could happen
To thousands of women, but I never thought
It could happen to somebody such as myself,
And then I heard me demanding justice
Whatever it took. Now it is taking
The rest of my life to come to nothing,
The rest of my life along with the rest.

What seems to be the problem is this:
That I was completely alone when it happened.
I don't mean alone in the room with him,
Alone with him – I mean really alone,
Alone with nothing. There was no witness.
I am a victim and cannot be witness.
One must play one role or the other.
If I bore witness I'd not be a victim,
He would be victim, if he had been there,
And if he'd been there then he would be witness
Against himself, but I was alone. Alone
With nothing. The window was open.

The wind and the rain were driving in,
The facts of life, lifting the curtains,
And I was asleep. I don't know when.

What happens now is I make a confession –
Confess, though I am the victim here,
To having the most incredible dreams
I believed were real, as long as they lasted;
To having had dreams I believed were ended
When the end was only a part of the dream,
The part where you wake in your own bedroom
Glad to be woken, till the door creaks
And whatever it was you were running from
Walks right in. I confess to recurring
Dreams in which my room is haunted
That seem more real than my waking life,
To a ghost who comes in the form of a pressure
Imprisoning me, by sternum and shoulders
And thighs, as if I were caught under glass.

Here you will ask if I ever protested,
Pushed him away, or cried for help,
If I fought my end, if I offered resistance
And made him aware of my lack of desire
With words he could readily comprehend,
In the face of his power, tearing my slip
Aside without touching, without coming near,
If I spoke though I was unable to speak
Or moved though I was unable to move,
Unable even to turn my head
In darkness, whether I happened to see

A distinguishing feature, or felt like revealing
If he was a stranger or someone I know,
And I'll tell you again that I witnessed nothing
More than I've mentioned, and nothing less.

I know what you're thinking. This isn't a crime.
A crime requires a perpetrator
To put in the dock, to accuse or defend,
To finish the plot, but there's nobody here.
Years ago, there would have been bodies,
Physical bodies at which I could point
And call them up to account for their cells
Under my nails, their spit on my neck,
But now they've learned to walk through walls.
If I could give you a face or a name
We'd have a dynamic. And yet if I did,
This still would not be considered a crime
Of a certain order, but something less,
Something one should take on the chin,
Something that could have been worse.

Now, am I sleeping, or am I awake?
This court seems more like the court of a dream
I visit each night, improperly dressed,
In which I am doomed to repeat myself
And in the repeating I doom myself
Before these hundred unfriendly faces
To find no relief in the drop of the gavel
Which never arrives. A dream alright,
A dream of running. The limbs refuse,
The air resists with the slowness of water,

The mind outpaces the body and sees
A child falling, but fails to react,
As I saw what was coming but failed to react,
Locked inside my sleeping body.
I'll never release myself from that.

MOON

Startled by the moon in the middle of the day,
same blue as the sky, like a crater in it,
for the first time in years I think of the flag
still flying there, of the men whose lives are fastened to it
even though the rest of us have turned away,

and I think of all the places I've been
in love, or happy, where I'll never go again
and probably couldn't find – that linden tree in Boston
I was lying under, watching summer's college kids
lope across the grass on their muscled brown legs,
when I suddenly headed for home.

There are bones inside my body I've never seen.

WHAT WILL IT BE TO BE OLD?

Waking stiff
at five o'clock
I hear a ghost keel
my own cool pelvis
creak

SHEEP SKULL

Stump of a horn, crater of an eye, dints, hollows and
    hairline cracks,
Grooved teeth with triple points that click in the long-dry
    runners of the jaw
Now the gums have gone back. Holes for drainage and
    handling pressure
In the open system of the head, closely packed as
    orchestral instruments'
Resonating-chambers and pipes. Ending abruptly in the
    absence of a neck.

Thoughts gather, as the flies once gathered: helping dip the
    sheep as a child,
Helping without helping, just greasing my hands on their coats
    as they passed
From one enclosure into the next. Them sensing a danger and
    doubling back
Against the barred gates their cumbersome bodies, the blunt of
    their heads.
Some drowning in only a foot of dip as the other sheep
    trampled them down.

ASHES

They're raked out cool and soft as crumbled silk,
tipping from the hearth's brass spade on to newsprint,
more than expected, each log finely dense
in dispersion – the wrapped weight, the moment,
of a baby in your arms – then out
to the garden's bonfire heap, to burn again
with the season's wrecked tree, but the wind
blows the folded paper open. There they go:
grey stream above the winter pond, purposeful,
fanned, reaching-for; a trick, of course, but something
held, like dust that looks to travel up the light.

GLISS

Those Sunday mornings, surfacing to find
the futon bigger and his pillow cold,
I confess to feeling a second's relief
as I shifted, pleasantly half-asleep,
back to the solo self I'd always been;
until the tuning-up began again
from the living room, where he sat alone
bending every errant note back into shape;

then troubling between two chords he loved
the silver shriek of a hand on the move,
that tell, that banshee of art-in-creation
they call a *gliss*: a slight imperfection's
imperfect name, just shy of *glitch* or *loss*,
and not quite *bliss*, as it never quite is.

IN THE BEGINNING

In the beginning he thought of the end.
Submitting a kiss to her dry mouth,
he remembered the end of other beginnings
too fresh in his mind,
freshly-dug holes where the soil stays dark,
spoiling the garden. They kissed in the garden
belonging to a friend, and then on the sofa
he was thinking of the end:
the kiss and the thought were inevitable,
were both the same being,
the fact of the end before it began
contained in the pleasure of kissing her mouth.
Once he had slugged, at the height of summer,
a cold can and taken a sting
from the wasp inside, that had crawled right in
to suckle the sugar. Did she feel the same?
Surely she did, but she didn't let on.
He was alone in foreseeing the end
and couldn't foretell
if that made it more or less likely to come,
if, by even thinking about it,
he made it more or less likely to come,
her cooling off, like an evening garden
when the sun takes back its heat from the air,
distant and unstoppable,
by increments hardly worth commenting upon,
until it was over, beginning and end,
until the end of the end had come.

Don't think, he thought, kissing her again:
dry lips and a cold tongue.
Would they lie down? – no, not yet.
Would she refuse him? Would they meet up?
And where would they go and what would they do
if the casual conversation was slow
and she saw his unease like a shopping trolley exposed
on the riverbed at the height of summer
when the water-level drops unusually low?
He knew in the end
he would remember the beginning,
how perfect it was, how perfectly slow, there on the sofa,
her lips and his lips coming together
for what seemed like ages, enough to consider
her lips were dry and her tongue was cold
and that didn't matter. It seemed
like forever, her mouth in the darkness
where now he's alone
and has been alone for what seems like forever.

LOOKOUT

Nothing in sight but water's deferrals,
deflections, its million-galloned grief;
though sometimes, when the light is angled so
as to prism inside the waves' tips,
it seems we're actually anchored in fields:
that we could drop off and land on our feet
in a rich plough-land confected with frost,
in mud flats, or sand dunes. We could forget
dry land is a dream in the dream of it.

THE GAPS

And then they revealed that solids were not solid
That a wall was not solid
That it consisted of molecules fixed and vibrating
Some distance apart, as did the flesh

That solidity was really the likelihood
Of stuff not falling
Between two chairs, down the gaps

And that walking through the wall was not impossible
That it could be like
Slipping between pine trunks into a forest
Which had looked from the road impermeable
But was where something lived

And that one could peer back from the gloom towards the light
A different creature
With tender eyes, with an ear for water

SIGHT

That winter drift-trapped in the house,
learning the campfire of flesh and the endless
tether the mind ranges upon,

I came into the living room and saw
a glass jug suspended in the air, six feet clear
of the carpet, tipped. There were no wires,

no mirror tricks. The whole world hung
on whatever invisible hook or hand
was keeping it tilted, empty, gleaming.

I stepped towards it, as if in a dream. It fell
as the rain falls, suddenly out of
the sky's indifference, and shattered at once.

THE GREY LADY

Her movements are recorded here,
the corridor a susceptible ribbon
crimped and spooled inside a cassette,

where she takes her slow promenade
and flickers, a dud transmitter knocked
at the selfsame instant, the selfsame spot.

Translucent as *shoji*, opal glass
in a shower door, your own steamy breath,
beneath her gown's embroidery

the world remains; the wallpaper's
grain is like gravel through water
and her a wave travelling along;

or she is what floats inside the wave
as it fills a pool: something else
of a piece with the water,

something distinct, but hardly there,
like wet tissue blossoming,
each tender frond a temperature-change

over the stones they barely obscure:
a suggestion, a sort of visitor
only certain attitudes of light

permit you to see. She brings no report
but veiled spaces of outlying water,
transparencies within transparencies.

IMMORTALITY

At the market stall
I pay four pounds for my name
to be written on a grain of rice,

each letter so small
I myself cannot read it
even though I know it's there,

or, am led
to believe it's there
by the old man's labour with needles
and chopsticks,

the diffident way
he pockets his fee
like one better paid by the moment's work.

THE FORTUNE TELLER

This is the second-oldest profession.
Since time out of memory, I have sat
in a small room at the turn of the stairs,
listening to them clamber towards me –
men and women, old and young, all breathless
in the thin, cold air of the divine.
They push their hands through the beaded curtain's
long strands that sway with a rosary click
between the compulsory world and mine,
where I wait behind the wooden table
winding and unwinding my deck of cards
from their dealing-cloth, a length of velvet
faded to pink on one side by the sun.
Come in, I say. *Don't be afraid. I won't*
tell you anything you'd rather not know.
It's always the future they ask about –
if the sick will recover, or the lost
turn into the driveway one afternoon,
recognizable and full of remorse.
Simple minds, that think what's coming next
is as distinct from what preceded it
as the sudden and unwarranted win
or loss on those lottery scratch-cards
they buy each evening, with fluttering nerves,
as if the life they deserve is waiting
in womblike darkness on the other side
of the silver foil. *There's been a mistake*

that will in good time be rectified.
Take them to court and you'll get it all back.
Your lover isn't callous, he's afraid.
Instead of this, I could tell them the Greeks
imagined walking backwards through their lives
as if up a steepening mountain path,
gaining both distance and altitude
until what they'd suffered through lay revealed
in its true proportion and character
on the valley floor and in the foothills
where once they were lost in a wood, or trapped
in the tiny settlements of their youth
when the world was nothing more than a white
boredom of high walls and elderly men
dreaming in the shade of the cypress trees.
Most important was to understand
where you had come from and how you had been
so tender-footed, so rash, so afraid
of the girls weaving ivy in their hair,
and the ram's horns growing out of his head
like wisdom with a format of its own,
that you had squandered chances as they came –
not to strain your neck for a second's glimpse
of the summit that may or may not be
behind you, for which so many mistook
a late quarry-lip or an early ridge.
But the clients grow impatient with this.
They are paying, and I should perform
whatever dance confirms their little hopes,
which are, in the final analysis,

just as heartstoppingly predictable
as those of people centuries before
who needed a good harvest, or a son
to stop the neighbour buying up their land.
When the hour is over, and they vanish
back down the stairwell, buttoning their coats,
I twitch the netting away from the glass
and watch for them to reappear below
as children wait for thrown sticks to emerge
from underneath the darkness of a bridge,
spinning in momentary vortices,
caught in a cap of scum, or somehow free
to race toward the foaming cataract;
and though home lies in a fixed direction
I see them look around, and hesitate,
feeling their pockets for something lost
which up till now they hadn't even missed.
My skill, you understand, is only this.

THE GREAT BEAR

A clear night
Trying to understand
What happened all those years ago
Under this
Exact constellation.

It does no good
To dwell on the past.
What happens happens only once.
No such thing
As a lesson can be learned.

And yet the same figure
Slowly appears
At the foot of the garden,
Looking as if
He is made of the dark,

And I feel the same
Dilemmas rise
That have risen before,
And the same reactions
Hours behind,

Burning off
What I've made of my life.
By the time the starlight reaches us
The world it began
Has gone.

CLEAN

Hung as long as your Granny suggested,
over the year-cusp, so its unassuming death
bridged the gap we open for ourselves
between the way we live and what we want,

we took the pheasant back into the woods.
I swear I've never known a peace like this:
the pretty wings tossed on the compost heap,
likewise the legs, and the loose-hanging head,

everything superfluous trimmed down
to a man and a woman, side by side,
hollowing out the body's opened fist
and finding lodged in the stomach sack

a moor-tangle, still brilliant green;
peace that the future doesn't concern us,
the last of its membranes rinsing away
under the cold tap as the meat came clean.

SCANDINAVIA

I think I could be happy there, north of fame, in light
unbroken, blending the imagined hours' horizons into sky, sky
through soft-heaped fields, unclaimed, their rims forever
reforming at the wind's deft caprice. I could try

to live as a glass of water, utterly clear and somehow
restrained, a sip that tells you nothing
but perpetuates the being-there; could sit, lie, settle down,
    the white
of one idea entirely lost upon another, as rain is lost

in the shift of the sea, as a single consecrated face
drowns in the swell of the Saturday host, and the notion of
    loving
that one critically more than any other flake in a flurry
melts, flows back to folly's pool, the lucid public dream.